Collins

Reading Comprehension Progress Tests

Year 1 / P2

Author:
Shelley Welsh

Series editor:
Stephanie Austwick

William Collins's dream of knowledge for all began with the publication of his first book in 1819.

A self-educated mill worker, he not only enriched millions of lives, but also founded a flourishing publishing house. Today, staying true to this spirit, Collins books are packed with inspiration, innovation and practical expertise. They place you at the centre of a world of possibility and give you exactly what you need to explore it.

Collins. Freedom to teach.

Published by Collins
An imprint of HarperCollins*Publishers*
The News Building
1 London Bridge Street
London
SE1 9GF

Browse the complete Collins catalogue at
www.collins.co.uk

© HarperCollins*Publishers* Limited 2019

10 9 8 7 6 5 4 3 2 1

ISBN 978-0-00-833342-3

British Library Cataloguing-in-Publication Data

A catalogue record for this publication is available from the British Library.

Author: Shelley Welsh

Series editor: Stephanie Austwick

Publisher: Katie Sergeant

Product Manager: Catherine Martin

Development editor: Judith Walters

Copyeditor and typesetter: Hugh Hillyard-Parker

Proofreader: Catherine Dakin

Cover designers: The Big Mountain Design, Ken Vail Graphic Design

Production controller: Katharine Willard

Printed and bound by CPI Group (UK) Ltd, Croydon, CR0 4YY

The publishers gratefully acknowledge the permission granted to reproduce the copyright material in this book. Every effort has been made to trace copyright holders and to obtain their permission for the use of copyright material. The publishers will gladly receive any information enabling them to rectify any error or omission at the first opportunity.

TEXT

An extract on pp.12-14 from *New from Old: Recycling Plastic* reprinted by permission of HarperCollins Publishers Ltd © 2011 Anthony Robinson; An extract on pp.21-23 from *Crunch and Munch* reprinted by permission of HarperCollins Publishers Ltd © 2007 Nora Sands; An extract on pp.32-35 from *Big Cat Babies* reprinted by permission of HarperCollins Publishers Ltd © 2005 Jonathan and Angela Scott

IMAGES

pp.7,9 &10 © HarperCollins Publishers Ltd 2019; p.12 Green Leaf/Shutterstock; p.13l suteelak phundang/Shutterstock; p.13r Elena Elisseeva/Shutterstock; p.14 Citizen of the Planet/Alamy Stock Photo; p.16 © HarperCollins Publishers Ltd 2019; p.21t Photo by Véronique Leplat reprinted by permission of HarperCollins Publishers Ltd © HarperCollins Publishers Ltd 2007; p.21b Africa Studio/Shutterstock; p.23 Photo by Véronique Leplat reprinted by permission of HarperCollins Publishers Ltd © HarperCollins Publishers Ltd 2007; pp.25,26,27 & 29 © HarperCollins Publishers Ltd 2019; pp.32,34 & 35 Reprinted by permission of HarperCollins Publishers Ltd © Jonathan and Angela Scott 2005; pp.36 & 37 © HarperCollins Publishers Ltd 2019.

MIX
Paper from
responsible sources
FSC
www.fsc.org **FSC™ C007454**

This book is produced from independently certified FSC paper
to ensure responsible forest management.

For more information visit:
www.harpercollins.co.uk/green

Contents

How to use this book

Introduction

Collins *Reading Comprehension Progress Tests* have been designed to give you a consistent whole-school approach to teaching and assessing reading comprehension. Each photocopiable book covers the required reading comprehension objectives from the 2014 Primary English National Curriculum. For teachers in Scotland, the books can offer guidance and structure that is not provided in the Curriculum for Excellence Experiences and Outcomes or Benchmarks.

As standalone tests, independent of any teaching and learning scheme, Collins *Reading Comprehension Progress Tests* provide a structured way to assess progress in reading comprehension skills, to help you identify areas for development, and to provide evidence towards expectations for each year group.

Assessment of higher order reading skills

At the end of Key Stage 1 and Key Stage 2, children are assessed on their ability to demonstrate reading comprehension. This is done through national tests (SATs) accompanied by teacher assessment. The Collins *Reading Comprehension Progress Tests* have been designed to provide children with opportunities to explore a range of texts whilst building familiarity with the format, language and style of the SATs. Using the tests with your classes each half-term will offer you a snapshot of your pupils' progress throughout the year.

The tests draw on a wide range of text types, from original stories and poems to engaging non-fiction material. The questions follow the style and format of SATs papers at a level appropriate to the year group. The tests provide increasing challenge within each year group and across the school. Regular use of the progress tests should help children to develop and practise the necessary skills required to complete the national tests with confidence.

How to use this book

In this book, you will find six photocopiable half-termly tests. You will also find a Curriculum Map on page 6 indicating the elements of the Content Domain covered in each test and across the year group. These have been cross-referenced with the appropriate age-related statements from the National Curriculum.

These Year 1 tests demonstrate some of the standard SAT-style questions and the format and layout of Key Stage 1 Reading Paper 1, where the text is presented in shorter sections with integrated questions, making it more manageable for the reader. Tests 1–4 use a single text and carry a total of 10 marks. Tests 5 and 6, ideally delivered in the Summer Term, contain two contrasting texts and carry a total of 20 marks. There is no set amount of time for completion of these tests.

Initially, in Year 1, you may prefer to deliver these tests with individuals or small groups, encouraging children to develop in confidence and independence. You may also wish to use the tests to teach retrieval skills and to model how to answer the various styles of question. To help you mark the tests, you will find mark schemes that include the number of marks to be awarded, model answers and a reference to the elements of the Content Domain covered by each question.

Test demand

The tests have been written to ensure smooth progression in children's reading comprehension within the book and across the rest of the books in the series. Each test builds on those before it so that children are guided towards the expectations of the SATs at the end of KS1 and KS2.

Year group	Test	Number of texts per test	Length of text per test	Number of marks per test
1	Autumn 1	1	80–100 words	10
1	Autumn 2	1	80–100 words	10
1	Spring 1	1	80–100 words	10
1	Spring 2	1	80–100 words	10
1	Summer 1	2	Up to 200 words in total	20
1	Summer 2	2	250 words each or 500 words in total	20

Performance thresholds

The table below provides guidance for assessing how children perform in the tests. Most children should achieve scores at or above the expected standard with some children working at greater depth and exceeding expectations for their year group. Whilst these threshold bands do not represent standardised scores, as in the end of key stage SATs, they will give an indication of how pupils are performing against the expected standard for their year group.

Year group	Test	Working towards	Expected	Greater depth
2	Autumn 1	5 marks or below	6–7 marks	8–10 marks
2	Autumn 2	5 marks or below	6–7 marks	8–10 marks
2	Spring 1	5 marks or below	6–7 marks	8–10 marks
2	Spring 2	5 marks or below	6–7 marks	8–10 marks
2	Summer 1	10 marks or below	11–15 marks	16–20 marks
2	Summer 2	10 marks or below	11–15 marks	16–20 marks

Tracking progress

A record sheet is provided to help you illustrate to children the areas in which their reading comprehension is strong and where they need to develop. A spreadsheet tracker is also provided via **collins.co.uk/assessment/downloads** which enables you to identify whole-class patterns of attainment. This can be used to inform your next teaching and learning steps.

Editable download

All the files are available online in Word and PDF format. Go to **collins.co.uk/assessment/downloads** to find instructions on how to download. The files are password-protected and the password clue is included on the website. You will need to use the clue to locate the password in your book.

You can use the editable Word files to help you meet the specific needs of your class, whether that be by increasing or decreasing the challenge, by reducing the amount of questions, by providing more space for answers or increasing the size of text for specific children.

Year 1 Curriculum map: Yearly overview

National Curriculum objective (Year 1)	Content domain	Test 1	Test 2	Test 3	Test 4	Test 5		Test 6	
		Fiction	Non-fiction	Poetry	Fiction	Fiction	Poetry	Non-fiction	Fiction
Link what they read to their own experiences.	1d Make inferences from the text.	●	●	●	●	●	●	●	●
Discuss word meanings and link new meanings to words already known.	1a Draw on knowledge of vocabulary to understand texts.	●	●	●	●	●	●	●	●
Draw on what they already know or on background information and vocabulary provided.	1a Draw on knowledge of vocabulary to understand texts.	●	●	●	●	●	●	●	●
	1d Make inferences from the text.	●	●	●	●	●	●	●	●
	1e Predict what might happen on the basis of what has been read so far.	●	●	●	●	●	●	●	●
Discuss the significance of the title and events.	1b Identify/explain key aspects of fiction and non-fiction texts, such as characters, events, titles and information.	●	●	●	●	●	●	●	●
	1c Identify and explain the sequence of events in texts.	●	●	●	●	●			●
Make inferences from the text based on what is said or done.	1d Make inferences from the text.	●		●	●	●			●
Predict what might happen from what has been read so far.	1e Predict what might happen on the basis of what has been read so far.	●					●	●	●
Identify/explain key aspects of fiction and non-fiction texts, such as characters, events, titles and information.	1b Identify/explain key aspects of fiction and non-fiction texts, such as characters, events, titles and information.	●	●	●	●		●	●	●
	1c Identify and explain the sequence of events in texts.	●	●	●	●	●	●	●	●

Name: Class: Date:

Breakfast at Mia's

by Shelley Welsh

Mia woke up at 7 o'clock. She listened to the sounds in the kitchen.

The dog snoring. *Grumph!*

Dad filling the kettle with water. *Splash!*

Mum laying the table. *Clunk!*

"Breakfast is ready, Mia!" said Mum.

Mia ran downstairs to the kitchen.

1 What did Mia hear when she woke up?

✓ Tick **one**.

the noise from the traffic outside ☐

the alarm clock ringing ☐

children playing outside ☐

sounds from the kitchen ☐

◯
1 mark

2 Draw **three** lines to match what Mia heard to the sounds they made.

Mum laying the table	•	•	Grumph!
the dog snoring	•	•	Splash!
Dad filling the kettle	•	•	Clunk!

◯
1 mark

3 Who says, "Breakfast is ready, Mia!"?

_____

◯
1 mark

Mia drank a glass of milk. *Gulp!*

Dad poured a cup of tea for him and Mum.

"Mmm!" said Mum.

"Mmm!" said Dad.

4 What noise did Mia make when she drank her milk?

_____

1 mark

5 Why do you think Mum and Dad went *"Mmm!"* when they drank the tea?

✓ Tick **one**.

They liked the tea. ☐

They didn't like the tea. ☐

The tea was too cold. ☐

The tea was too hot. ☐

1 mark

Mum put some bread in the toaster.

When the toast was ready, it popped up. *Ping!*

6 How do you know the toast was ready?

_____

○

1 mark

Mum spread butter and jam on the toast with a knife.

"Yummy!" said Mia. The toast was crispy. She licked her lips. The jam had made them sticky.

"Now run upstairs and get ready for school!" said Mum.

7 Write **two** things that Mum put on Mia's toast.

1. _____

2. _____

◯ 2 marks

8 How do you know Mia enjoyed her toast?

_____

◯ 1 mark

9 Number the sentences below from **1** to **4**
to show the order in which they happened.

The first has been done for you.

Mia ate her toast.   ☐

Mia's mum put the bread in the toaster.   ☐

Mia went downstairs to the kitchen.   1

Mia drank a glass of milk.   ☐

◯ 1 mark

Name: Class: Date:

From **New from Old** – Recycling Plastic

by Anthony Robinson

What is recycling?

Recycling is making something new from something that has already been used.

Instead of throwing things away, we can collect and recycle them to make new things.

We can recycle glass, metal, plastic and paper.

1 What is recycling?   ✓ Tick **one**.

Making something old from something new. ☐

Throwing away old things. ☐

Making something new from something
that has already been used. ☐

Collecting new things. ☐

1 mark

2 What can we do instead of throwing things away?

✓ Tick **one**.

Collect and recycle. ☐

Collect and throw away. ☐

Buy new things. ☐

Don't buy new things. ☐ ◯

1 mark

3 Write **two** things that we can recycle.

1. _____

2. _____ ◯

2 marks

How do we recycle plastic?

First we collect the plastic.

Then it is cut into small bits and washed.

Then the plastic is melted into pellets.

Now the old plastic can be used again.

We can make many things out of recycled plastic:

- clothes
- furniture
- toys.

Why is it good to recycle?

Too much rubbish is bad for the planet.

---

4 Number the sentences below from **1** to **4** to show the order in which they happen.

The first has been done for you.

The plastic is melted into pellets. ☐

The plastic is cut into small bits and washed. ☐

The plastic is collected. 1

The old plastic can be used again. ☐

1 mark

5 Write **two** things that can be made out of recycled plastic.

1. _____

2. _____   ◯

2 marks

6 What is bad for the planet?

_____   ◯

1 mark

7 Write **two** things that you recycle at home or at school.

1. _____

2. _____   ◯

2 marks

Name: Class: Date:

Weather
by Shelley Welsh

I like to hear the rain on the roof
When I am dry inside.
Pitter patter, pitter patter.
It's hammering on the roof.

I like to watch the snow fall softly
When I am warm indoors.
Whirling twirling, whirling twirling.
It's falling softly, falling softly.

I like to listen to the whistling wind
When I am snug inside.
Whooshing whooshing, whooshing
   whooshing.
It's blowing wildly through the trees.

I like to see the shimmering sunshine
When it's nice and warm outdoors.
Shining, shimmering, shining,
   shimmering.
It's such fun when I play in the sun!

Read **Verse 1**.

1 Where does the writer like to be when it is raining outside?

✓ Tick **one**.

outside ☐

inside ☐

on the roof ☐

in the garden ☐ ◯ 1 mark

2 What does the word *hammering* tell you?

✓ Tick **one**.

that the rain is noisy ☐

that someone is working on the roof ☐

that the rain is falling quietly ☐

that the roof has a leak ☐ ◯ 1 mark

Read **Verse 2**.

3 Write **one** word that describes how the snow falls.

_____ ◯ 1 mark

Read **Verse 3**.

4 *When I am snug indoors.*

Choose another word that means the same as *snug*.

✓ Tick **one**.

sleepy ☐

cosy ☐

chilly ☐

bored ☐

1 mark

5 Where is the wind blowing?

_____

1 mark

Read **Verse 4**.

6 *It's such fun to play in the sun!*

Which **two** words in this line rhyme?

_____ and _____

1 mark

Look at the **whole** poem.

7 Put ticks (✓) in the table to show which of these are **true** and which are **false**.

Sentence	True	False
The writer likes to play in the sun.		
The snow whirls and twirls as it falls.		
The wind blows gently.		

1 mark

8 Draw **three** lines to match the words that have similar meanings.

One has been done for you.

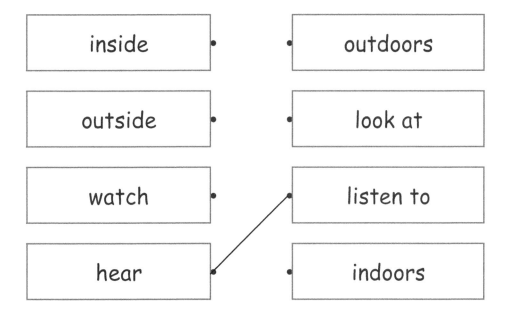

inside	outdoors
outside	look at
watch	listen to
hear	indoors

1 mark

9 Draw **three** lines to match what the writer sees and hears in the **whole** poem.

One has been done for you.

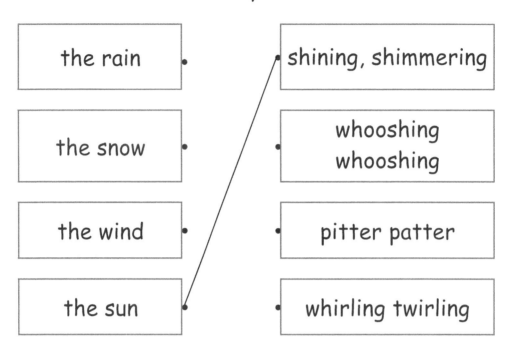

1 mark

10 Number the sentences below from **1** to **4** to show the order in which they happen in the poem.

The first has been done for you.

The writer has fun in the sun. ☐

The writer is snug inside. ☐

The rain is hammering on the roof. 1

The snow falls softly. ☐

1 mark

Name: Class: Date:

From **Crunch and Munch**

by Nora Sands

Rainbow Kebabs

Here are some fruit kebabs to make your tastebuds tingle.

What you need:

* wooden skewers

* any type of washed fruit, such as:

- apples   - raspberries

- bananas   - kiwis

- oranges   - strawberries

- grapes   - grapefruit

1 What type of text is *Crunch and Munch*?

✓ Tick **one**.

a story ☐

a letter ☐

instructions ☐

an invitation ☐

1 mark

2 What will the Rainbow Kebabs do to your tastebuds?

_____

1 mark

3 **Find** and **copy** the names of **two** fruits you could use to make Rainbow Kebabs.

1. _____

2. _____

2 marks

* For a sauce: • yoghurt • honey

What to do:

1. Choose your fruit.

2. Peel or remove the skin if you need to.

3. Cut the large fruit into bite-sized chunks.

4. If you have chosen oranges or grapefruit, separate the segments.

5. Small fruit like strawberries, raspberries and grapes don't need to be cut.

6. Push the fruit chunks carefully onto the wooden skewers, in any order you like.

7. Then mix up some yoghurt and honey in a little bowl … dip, and eat!

4 What **two** ingredients do you need for the sauce?

1. _____

2. _____

2 marks

5 What might you do to the fruit skin?

_____

◯

1 mark

6 Draw **four** lines to match the ingredients with the instructions.

large fruit	Separate the segments.
small fruit	Mix in a little bowl.
yoghurt and honey	Don't cut them up.
oranges and grapefruit	Cut into bite-sized chunks

◯

1 mark

7 Read steps **3** and **6**.

Explain why you will need an adult to help you.

Step **3**: _____

_____

Step **6**: _____

_____

◯

2 marks

Name: Class: Date:

Hansel and Gretel

by Shelley Welsh

Once there was a boy and a girl called Hansel and Gretel. They lived with their father and their unkind stepmother.

They were poor and had very little food.

"Those children eat too much! Get rid of them!" their stepmother said to their dad.

1 Write one word that tells you that Hansel and Gretel's stepmother wasn't very nice.

_____

1 mark

2 Why do you think the stepmother wanted to get rid of Hansel and Gretel?

_____

○ 1 mark

3 Which word tells you that the family didn't have much money?

_____

○ 1 mark

So the children's dad took them into a deep dark forest and left them there.

The children came to a little cottage made of sweets, cakes, ice cream and chocolate!

Hansel knocked on the sugary door.

4 Do you think the forest seemed scary? Why?

_____

○ 1 mark

5 What was different about the cottage?

_____

1 mark

6 Which word describes the cottage door?

✓ Tick **one**.

little ☐

sugary ☐

sweet ☐

wooden ☐

1 mark

7 How do you think Hansel felt when he knocked on the cottage door? Why?

_____

_____

2 marks

An old woman with a pointy nose appeared. "What bony birds! You won't take long in the oven." And she shoved them into a cage!

8 **Copy** one word to fill in the gap below.

When the door opened, an old woman

with a _____ nose stood there.

bony   pointy   sharp   small

1 mark

9 Why does the old woman think that Hansel and Gretel look like bony birds?

_____

_____

1 mark

10 What do you think the old woman wants to do with Hansel and Gretel? Why do you think that?

_____

_____

_____

2 marks

My Brother Billy
by Shelley Welsh

My little brother Billy
Is often very silly.
He pretends he is an aeroplane
Or else a noisy steam train.

One day he said he was a bear
And climbed up onto Mummy's chair.
He bared his teeth and let out a roar
Then landed "THUD!" upon the floor.

Once he said he was a spider.
He spread his arms so he was wider
And tried to crawl up the kitchen wall,
But all he did was slip and fall.

Today Billy is a little boy
Who likes to play with all his toys.
When I pretended to be a bee,
He simply wouldn't look at me.

Read **Verse 1**.

11 How does Billy make himself look like an aeroplane?

_____

○ 1 mark

Read **Verse 2**.

12 What do the words _He bared his teeth_ mean?

✓ Tick **one**.

He showed his teeth. ☐

He licked his teeth. ☐

He brushed his teeth. ☐

He gnashed his teeth. ☐

○ 1 mark

13 Why did Billy _let out a roar?_

_____

○ 1 mark

Read **Verse 3**.

14 What happened when Billy tried to be a spider?
Write **two** things.

1. _____

2. _____

○ 2 marks

15 Which word rhymes with *spider*?

_____

○ 1 mark

Look at the **whole** poem.

16 Put ticks (✓) in the table to show which of these are **true** and which are **false**.

Sentence	True	False
Billy is the writer's elder brother.		
Billy pretended to be a bee.		
Billy tried to crawl up the kitchen wall.		

○ 1 mark

17 Number the sentences below from **1** to **4** to show the order in which they happen.

The first has been done for you.

Billy falls with a thud to the floor. ☐

Billy plays with his toys. ☐

Billy pretends to be a steam train. 1

Billy climbs on Mummy's chair. ☐

○ 1 mark

Name:	Class:	Date:

From **Big Cat Babies**

by Jonathan and Angela Scott

In Africa there are wild places where the big cats live.

Africa's big cats are lions, cheetahs and leopards.

Lions live in a group called a pride.

Their babies are called cubs.

A female lion is called a lioness.

She keeps her cubs hidden until they can walk.

Cubs learn to live with the pride. Everyone helps to bring up the cubs.

1 Name **two** of Africa's big cats.

1. _____

2. _____

2 marks

2 Draw **three** lines to match the words on the left to a word on the right.

| group of lions | • | • | cub |

| female lion | • | • | lioness |

| baby lion | • | • | pride |

1 mark

3 How does a lioness protect her cubs until they can walk?

✓ Tick **one**.

She plays with them. ☐

She washes them. ☐

She hides them. ☐

She feeds them. ☐

1 mark

4 Put ticks (✓) in the table to show which of these are **true** and which are **false**.

Sentence	True	False
The whole pride brings up the lion cubs.		
Tigers are one of Africa's big cats.		
Africa's big cats live in wild places.		

1 mark

5 In the text, what is the name given to animals such as lions, leopards and cheetahs? Why?

_____

_____

_____

2 marks

Leopards live on their own.

They often live in woods where they can hide.

They like to go out at night.

Cheetahs hunt in the daytime.

They are the fastest animals in the world.

They must eat quickly when they kill. Other animals could steal their food.

6 Why are the woods a good place for leopards to live?

_____

1 mark

7 Who do leopards live with?

✓ Tick **one**.

They live with lions. ☐

They live on their own. ☐

They live with humans. ☐

They live with cheetahs. ☐

1 mark

8 Why do you think cheetahs are successful hunters?

_____

1 mark

Tilly's Kitten

by **Shelley Welsh**

Tilly was excited.

Dad was taking her to get a kitten!

Dad drove to a farm where there was a sign. KITTENS!

The farmer said, "Hello, do you want a kitten?"

"Yes, please," said Tilly.

The farmer took her to the barn.

There were four tiny kittens purring in the straw.

9 Why was Tilly excited?

✓ Tick **one**.

She was going to get a puppy. ☐

She was going to play on a farm. ☐

She was going to the park with her dad. ☐

She was going to get a kitten. ☐

1 mark

10 What were the kittens doing when Tilly first saw them?

_____ ◯

1 mark

"Which one would you like?" asked the farmer.

Tilly chose the tiniest kitten.

He looked like a little ball of shiny, black fur.

The farmer carefully picked up the kitten and placed him gently in Tilly's hands.

"I promise I will look after him," said Tilly.

The little kitten licked her hand with its pink tongue.

"I'm going to call him Snuggles," she said, and wrapped him in her scarf to keep him warm.

11 Which kitten did Tilly choose?

✓ Tick **one**.

the biggest ☐

the tiniest ☐

the eldest ☐

the youngest ☐

◯

1 mark

12 He looked like a little ball of shiny, black fur.

Why do you think he looked like this?

_____

◯

1 mark

13 Which **two** words tell you that the farmer cared about the kitten?

1. _____

2. _____

◯

2 marks

14 What did Tilly promise to do?

_____

◯

1 mark

15 Do you think Snuggles is a good name for a kitten? Circle **Yes** or **No** and give a reason.

Yes   **No**

_____

1 mark

16 How do you think Tilly feels at the end of the story? Why?

_____

_____

_____

2 marks

Mark scheme for Autumn Half Term Test 1

Qu.	Content domain	Requirement	Mark
		Breakfast at Mia's	
1	1b	**Award 1 mark** for sounds from the kitchen.	1
2	1a, 1b	**Award 1 mark** for all 3 lines correct: Mum laying the table — *Clunk!* the dog snoring — *Grumph!* Dad filling the kettle — *Splash!*	1
3	1b	**Award 1 mark** for Mum.	1
4	1b	**Award 1 mark** for *Gulp!*	1
5	1d	**Award 1 mark** for They liked the tea.	1
6	1d	**Award 1 mark** for it popped up / it went *Ping!*	1
7	1b	**Award 1 mark** for butter and **1 mark** for jam.	2
8	1d	**Award 1 mark** for she said, "Yummy!"	1
9	1c	**Award 1 mark** for all 4 numbers correct. 1 = Mia went downstairs to the kitchen. 2 = Mia drank a glass of milk. 3 = Mia's mum put the bread in the toaster. 4 = Mia ate her toast.	1
		TOTAL MARKS	**10**

Mark scheme for Autumn Half Term Test 2

Qu.	Content domain	Requirement	Mark
		New from Old: Recycling Plastic	
1	1b	**Award 1 mark** for Making something new from something that has already been used.	1
2	1b	**Award 1 mark** for Collect and recycle.	1
3	1b	**Award 1 mark** each for any 2 from: glass, metal, plastic and paper.	2
4	1c	1 = The plastic is collected. 2 = The plastic is cut into small bits and washed. 3 = The plastic is melted into pellets. 4 = The old plastic can be used again. **Award 1 mark** each for all three numbers correct.	1
5	1b	**Award 1 mark** each for any 2 from: clothes, furniture, toys.	2
6	1b	**Award 1 mark** for (too much) rubbish.	1
7	–	**Award 1 mark** each for any 2 examples: e.g. paper, bottles, plastic.	2
		TOTAL MARKS	**10**

Mark scheme for Spring Half Term Test 1

Qu.	Content domain	Requirement	Mark
		Weather	
1	1b	**Award 1 mark** for inside.	1
2	1d	**Award 1 mark** for that the rain is noisy.	1
3	1a	**Award 1 mark** for *softly*; also accept *whirling/twirling*.	1
4	1a	**Award 1 mark** for cosy.	1
5	1b	**Award 1 mark** for through the trees.	1
6	1b	**Award 1 mark** for both *fun* and *sun*.	1
7	1b	**Award 1 mark** for all answers correct: The writer likes to play in the sun – True. The snow whirls and twirls as it falls – True. The wind blows gently – False.	1
8	1a	**Award 1 mark** for all pairs correct: inside – indoors outside – outdoors watch – look at hear – listen to.	1
9	1b	**Award 1 mark** for all pairs correct: the rain – pitter patter the snow – whirling twirling the wind – whooshing whooshing the sun – shining, shimmering.	1
10	1c	**Award 1 mark** for all answers correct: 1 = The rain is hammering on the roof. 2 = The snow falls softly. 3 = The writer is snug inside. 4 = The writer has fun in the sun.	1
		TOTAL MARKS	10

Mark scheme for Spring Half Term Test 2

Qu.	Content domain	Requirement	Mark
		Crunch and Munch	
1	1b	**Award 1 mark** for instructions.	1
2	1a, 1b	**Award 1 mark** for (make them) tingle.	1
3	1b	**Award 1 mark** for any 2 from: apples raspberries bananas kiwis oranges strawberries grapes grapefruit	2
4	1b	**Award 1 mark** for yoghurt and **1 mark** for honey.	2
5	1b	**Award 1 mark** for peel it; remove the skin.	1
6	1b	**Award 1 mark** for all 4 lines correct: large fruit – Cut into bite-sized chunks. small fruit – Don't cut them up. yoghurt and honey – Mix in a little bowl. oranges and grapefruit – Separate the segments.	1
7	1d	**Award 1 mark** for each step correctly explained: Step 3: reference to cutting fruit; knife; dangerous. Step 6: reference to pointed skewer; sharp; dangerous.	2
		TOTAL MARKS	10

Mark scheme for Summer Half Term Test 1

Qu.	Content domain	Requirement	Mark
		Hansel and Gretel	
1	1a, 1b	**Award 1 mark** for *unkind*.	1
2	1b, 1d	**Award 1 mark** for she thought they ate too much; the family was poor; they had very little food. Also accept: she didn't like them; she was not very nice; she wanted the food for herself.	1
3	1a, 1b	**Award 1 mark** for *poor*.	1
4	1a, 1d	**Award 1 mark** for either Yes or No with a suitable explanation, e.g. Yes, because it is deep and dark; Yes, because their dad left them there (alone). No, because they find a cottage made of sweets.	1
5	1b, 1d	**Award 1 mark** for it was made of sweets, cakes, ice cream and chocolate. Also accept any one of these for the mark to be awarded.	1
6	1a, 1b	**Award 1 mark** for *sugary*.	1
7	1a, 1d	**Award 1 mark** for a reasonable suggestion and **1 mark** for evidence from the text. Accept any answer that demonstrates understanding of the text, e.g. brave – because he didn't know who lived there; frightened – because they were lost.	2
8	1b	**Award 1 mark** for *pointy*.	1
9	1a, 1d	**Award 1 mark** for they are so little/tiny; thin/skinny.	1
10	1d	**Award 1 mark** for a reasonable suggestion and **1 mark** for evidence from the text, e.g. she wants to eat them because she says they won't take long in the oven.	2
		My Brother Billy	
11	1b	**Award 1 mark** for put his arms out like an aeroplane's wings.	1
12	1a	**Award 1 mark** for He showed his teeth.	1
13	1b, 1d	**Award 1 mark** for because he was pretending to be a bear.	1
14	1b, 1d	**Award 1 mark each** for 2 points from: he spread his arms out wide (like a spider's legs); he tried to crawl up the wall; he slipped and fell.	2
15	1a, 1b	**Award 1 mark** for *wider*.	1
16	1b	**Award 1 mark** for all 3 correct: Billy is the writer's elder brother – False. Billy pretended to be a bee – False. Billy tried to crawl up the kitchen wall – True.	1
17	1c	**Award 1 mark** for all 4 correct: 1 = Billy pretends to be a steam train. 2 = Billy climbs on Mummy's chair. 3 = Billy falls with a thud to the floor. 4 = Billy plays with his toys.	1
		TOTAL MARKS	20

Mark scheme for Summer Half Term Test 2

Qu.	Content domain	Requirement	Mark
		Big Cat Babies	
1	1b	**Award 1 mark** each for any 2 from: lions; cheetahs; leopards.	2
2	1a, 1b	**Award 1 mark** for all 3 lines correct: group of lions – pride / female lion – lioness / baby lion – cub.	1
3	1b	**Award 1 mark** for She hides them.	1
4	1b	**Award 1 mark** for all 3 answers correct: The whole pride brings up the lion cubs – True. / Tigers are one of Africa's big cats – False. / Africa's big cats live in wild places – True	1
5	1d	**Award 1 mark** for *big cats* and **1 mark** for a correct reason: e.g. they look like cats; they are much bigger than cats.	2
6	1b	**Award 1 mark** for saying they can hide there.	1
7	1d, 1e	**Award 1 mark** for They live on their own.	1
8	1d	**Award 1 mark** for they are so fast / the fastest animals in the world.	1
		Tilly's Kitten	
9	1b	**Award 1 mark** for She was going to get a kitten.	1
10	1b	**Award 1 mark** for purring; purring in the straw.	1
11	1b	**Award 1 mark** for the tiniest.	1
12	1a, 1d	**Award 1 mark** for any reasonable answer that refers to size or shape, e.g. he was so small; he was curled up.	1
13	1a	**Award 1 mark** each for *carefully*; *gently*.	2
14	1b	**Award 1 mark** for she promised to look after him.	1
15	1d	**Award 1 mark** for either Yes or No with any reasoned answer: Yes, because a kitten likes to snuggle; likes to snuggle in your arms. / No, because when it's older, it might not want to snuggle any more.	1
16	1d	**Award 1 mark** for a reasonable suggestion and **1 mark** for evidence from the text, e.g. happy because she has a new kitten.	2
		TOTAL MARKS	20

Name:	Class:

Year 1 Reading Comprehension Record Sheet

Tests	Mark	Total marks	Key skills to target
Autumn Half Term Test 1			
Autumn Half Term Test 2			
Spring Half Term Test 1			
Spring Half Term Test 2			
Summer Half Term Test 1			
Summer Half Term Test 2			